zigzag
LANGUAGE MASTERS

Let's Learn SPANISH

Written and edited by
Carol Watson and **Janet de Saulles**

Consultant
Maria Dolores Le Fanu

Illustrated by
Shelagh McNicholas

Contents

The consultant, Maria Dolores Le Fanu, was born and raised in Spain. She has a degree in Spanish and History of Art from the University of London, and teaches Spanish and English in England.

This edition published in 2002 by Zigzag Children's Books, an imprint of Chrysalis Children's Books plc. 64 Brewery Road, London N7 9NT

ISBN 1 903954 34 7 (hb)
ISBN 1 903954 36 3 (pb)

Every effort has been made to ensure none of the recommended websites in this book is linked to inappropriate material. However, due to the ever-changing nature of the Internet, the publishers regret they cannot take responsibility for future content of these websites.

About this book

In this book you will find out how to speak Spanish. You will meet the González family who will show you what to say in many different situations. Here they are to introduce themselves. Everything the González family says is written in Spanish and English. There is also a guide to pronouncing Spanish words.

¡Hola! Somos el Señor y la Señora González.
(Olla! Somoss el Senyor ee la Senyora Gonthaleth.)
Hello! We are Señor and Señora González.

¡Hola! Soy Miguel.
(Olla! Soy Miggel.)
Hello! I'm Miguel.

¡Hola! Soy Carmen.
(Olla! Soy Carmen.)
Hello! I'm Carmen.

INTERNET LINKS

How to speak Spanish

These notes will help you to use the pronunciation guide:

Say 'a' like the 'a' in 'bad'.   Say 'o' like the 'o' in 'top'.
Say 'e' like the 'e' in 'bed'.   Say 'oo' like the 'oo' in 'good'.
Say 'ay' like the 'ay' in 'say'. Say 'ch' like the 'ch' in 'church'.
Say 'ee' like the 'ee' in 'feet'. Say 'th' like the 'th' in 'thing'.

- 'B' is used for the Spanish 'v'.
- 'Ny' is used in the guide to make the sound of the Spanish 'ñ'.
- 'H' is used for the Spanish 'j' and is pronounced like the 'ch' in 'loch'.

¿Question marks?

When there is a question or exclamation mark at the end of a sentence, the Spanish also put an upside-down question or exclamation mark at the beginning of the sentence.

Speaking to people

When you speak to a close friend or a relative, you use **tú**. If there is more than one friend or relative, you use **vosotros** (or **vosotras** if the group is female only). When you speak to somebody you do not know very well, you use **usted**. If there is more than one person you use **ustedes**.

Accents

In general, the second to last syllable of a Spanish word is stressed. When a different syllable is stressed, it is marked by an accent.

Masculine and feminine words

In Spanish, some words are masculine and some are feminine. **La** in front of a word means that it is is feminine and **el** usually means that it is masculine. For example, 'house' is feminine in Spanish - '**la** casa', while 'book' is masculine - '**el** libro'.

When the word is plural, for example, books or houses, then it has **las** or **los** in front of it ('**las** casas' and '**los** libros'). **Las** is the feminine plural and **los** is the masculine plural.

Meeting people

In the evenings, the González family often goes to the town centre for a walk. When Spanish people meet somebody that they do not know very well, they use the polite form of Spanish. Children also use this polite form when they speak to people older than themselves.

To say 'How are you?' in polite Spanish you can use '¿Cómo está?'. If you are speaking to more than one person you can say '¿Cómo están?'.

Buenas noches, Señor Sánchez. ¿Cómo está?
(Bwennas nochess, Senyor Sancheth. Como esta?)
Good evening, Señor Sanchez. How are you?

Muy bien, gracias.
(Mwee bee-en, grathyas.)
Very well, thank you.

When you meet somebody you know well, you can say '¿Cómo estás?'. If you are talking to more than one friend you can say '¿Cómo estáis?'.

¡Hola! ¿Cómo estás?
(Olla! Como estas?)
Hello! How are you?

Bien, gracias.
(Bee-en, grathyas.)
Fine, thank you.

4

Carmen and Miguel meet two children they have seen once before.

¡Hola! ¿Cómo os llamáis?
(Olla. Como os yamayis?)
Hello. What are you called?

Me llamo Francisco.
(May yamo Franthisco.)
I'm called Francisco.

Nos llamamos Carmen y Miguel.
(Nos yamamos Carmen ee Miggel.)
We're called Carmen and Miguel.

Tengo diez años.
(Tengo deeyeth anyos.)
I'm ten years old.

¡Vámonos! ¡Hasta luego!
(Bamonos! Asta lwego!)
Let's go! See you later!

¿Nos vemos aquí mañana?
(Nos bemos akee manyanna?)
Shall we meet here tomorrow?

¡Yo también!
(Yo tambee-en!)
Me too!

De acuerdo. Hasta mañana.
(Day akwerdo. Asta manyanna.)
OK. See you tomorrow.

Meeting people words

buenas tardes
(bwennas tardes)
good afternoon/
good evening

buenos días
(bwennos dee-as)
good morning

adiós
(addyoss)
goodbye

¿y tú?
(ee too?)
and you?

bastante bien
(bastantay bee-en)
quite well

Making friends

On their way home from school, Carmen and Miguel talk to an English boy and girl who started at their school that day. They talk about their families and where they live.

Family words

la familia
(la fameelya)
family

los padres
(los padress)
parents

el padre
(el padray)
father

el abuelo
(el abwelo)
grandfather

el tío
(el tee-o)
uncle

la tía
(la tee-a)
aunt

la madre
(la madray)
mother

la abuela
(la abwela)
grandmother

la hermana
(la ermana)
sister

el hermano
(el ermano)
brother

el primo
(el preemo)
cousin (male)

la prima
(la preema)
cousin (female)

el hijo
(el i-ho)
son

la hija
(la i-ha)
daughter

Finding the way

Señora González has taken her children out for the day. Before they go home they decide to have something to eat at a nearby café.

Por favor señora, ¿hay un café por aquí?
(Por fabbor senyora, eye oon caffay por akee?)
Excuse me madam, is there a café near here?

¿Está lejos?
(Esta layhos?)
Is it far?

No.
(No.)
No.

Por allí y gire a la izquierda.
(Por ayee ee heeray ah la ithkeeyerda.)
Over there and turn left.

la cabina telefónica
(la cabeena telefonnika)
telephone box

la gasolinera
(la gasolinerra)
petrol station

los servicios
(los serbeethyos)
toilets

el buzón
(el boothon)
letter-box

Direction words

todo recto
(toddo recto)
straight on

frente a
(frentay ah)
opposite

al lado de
(al laddo day)
next to

a la derecha
(ah la deretcha)
on the right

a la izquierda
(ah la ithkeeyerda)
on the left

After their meal, they ask a man the way to the station.

On the way home, Carmen gets lost. Her mother tries to find her.

¿Dónde está la estación, por favor?
(Donday esta la estathyon, por fabbor?)
Where is the station, please?

Me he perdido.
(May ay perdeedo.)
I am lost.

¡No encuentro a mí hija!
(No encwentro ah mee i-ha!)
I can't find my daughter!

Está a la derecha.
(Esta ah la deretcha.)
It's on the right.

el aeropuerto
(el aeropwerto)
airport

el hospital
(el ospital)
hospital

la comisaría
(la comisareeya)
police station

sobre
(sobray)
on

en
(en)
in

hasta
(asta)
as far as

cerca de aquí
(therka day akee)
nearby

en coche
(en cochay)
by car

a pie
(ah peeyay)
on foot

la iglesia
(la iglessya)
church

Staying in a hotel or house

The Spanish often have the whole month of August as holiday. During this month the González family likes to go to different parts of Spain. This year they are staying in a hotel for the first week, and in a friend's house for the second.

Nos gustaría reservar una habitación para una semana.
(Nos goostareeya reserbar oona abitathyon parra oona semanna.)
We would like to book a room for one week.

Sí señores. ¿Qué desean ustedes?
(See senyores. Kay desayan oostedes?)
Yes, sir and madam. What would you like?

Una habitación doble con baño, por favor.
(Oona abitathyon dobblay con banyo, por fabbor.)
A double room with a bathroom, please.

¡Me gusta este hotel!
(May goosta estay otel!)
I like this hotel!

la almohada
(la almwadda)
pillow

la sábana
(la sabbanna)
sheet

el mozo
(el motho)
porter

el balcón
(el balkon)
balcony

la cama
(la camma)
bed

la casa
(la casa)
house

arriba
(areeba)
upstairs

el dormitorio
(el dormitorreeyo)
bedroom

el cuarto de baño
(el cwarto day banyo)
bathroom

la butaca
(la bootacca)
armchair

la sala de estar
(la salla day estar)
living room

el televisor
(el telebissor)
television set

el comedor
(el commedor)
dining room

la puerta
(la pwerta)
door

la cocina
(la cotheena)
kitchen

las contraventanas
(las contrabentannas)
shutters

la ventana
(la bentanna)
window

la mesa
(la messa)
table

la silla
(la seeya)
chair

Camping

The González family is spending the last week of August on a campsite. Most Spanish campsites provide electricity, so that the campers can watch television or enjoy themselves as they would at home.

Por favor, ¿se puede acampar aquí?
(Por fabbor, say pwedday acampar akee?)
Excuse me, may we camp here?

Tenemos dos tiendas y un remolque.
(Tenemos doss teeyendas ee oon remolkay.)
We have two tents and a caravan.

Nos gustaría quedarnos siete días.
(Nos goostareeya keddarnos syettay dee-as.)
We'd like to stay for seven days.

Sí, de acuerdo.
(See, day akwerdo.)
Yes, that's fine.

¿Dónde está la tienda del camping?
(Donday esta la teeyenda del camping?)
Where is the campsite shop?

Está por allá.
(Esta por ayah.)
It's over there.

Por favor, ¿pueden hacer un poco menos de ruido?
(Por fabbor, pwedden ather oon poco mennos day rooeedo?)
Please could you make a little less noise?

Some more useful camping words and phrases

agua potable
(agwa potahblay)
drinking water

reservado para remolques
(reserbahdo parra remolkays)
caravans only

agua no potable
(agwa no potahblay)
non-drinking water

la tela impermeable
(la tella impermayabblay)
groundsheet

el camping
(el camping)
campsite

la tienda de campaña
(la teeyenda day campanya)
tent

el palo de la tienda
(el pallo day la teeyenda)
tent pole

el camping gas
(el camping gas)
camping gas

la estaca de la tienda
(la estacca day la teeyenda)
tent peg

el saco de dormir
(el sacco day dormeer)
sleeping bag

las duchas
(las doochas)
showers

el mazo
(el matho)
mallet

el colchón neumático
(el colchon newmattico)
airbed

¿Dónde están los servicios, por favor?
(Donday estan los serbeethyos, por fabbor?)
Where are the toilets, please?

Lo siento, ni idea.
(Lo seeyento, nee iday-ah.)
I'm sorry, I've no idea.

Están al lado de la tienda del camping.
(Estan al laddo day la teeyenda del camping.)
They are next to the campsite shop.

Going shopping

In most parts of Spain, the shops are open from 9 in the morning until 2 in the afternoon. They open again at 5 and close for the day at 8 in the evening.

¿Puedo ayudarle?
(Pweddo ayoodahlay?)
Can I help you?

Querría dos panes, por favor.
(Kerreeya doss pannes, por fabbor.)
I would like two loaves, please.

Food words

la leche
(la lechay)
milk

la mantequilla
(la mantekeeya)
butter

el yogurt
(el yogoort)
yoghurt

el huevo
(el webo)
egg

la patata
(la patatta)
potato

la col
(la coll)
cabbage

el tomate
(el tomattay)
tomato

la naranja
(la naranha)
orange

la manzana
(la manthanna)
apple

la carne
(la carnay)
meat

el pollo
(el pollo)
chicken

el azúcar
(el athoocar)
sugar

la mermelada
(la mermeladda)
jam

la carnicería
(la carnithereeya)
butcher's shop

el supermercado
(el supermercaddo)
supermarket

la panadería
(la pannadereeya)
bakery

Although the Spanish like to go to their local shops, supermarkets are being used more and more.

¿Cuánto es?
(Cwanto ess?)
How much is it?

Doce euros.
(Dothay ayuros.)
Twelve euros.

¿Desea algo más?
(Desaya algo mass?)
Would you like anything else?

Un kilo de tomates, por favor.
(Oon keelo day tomattess, por fabbor.)
A kilo of tomatoes, please.

la farmacia
(la farmathiya)
chemist's shop

la librería
(la librereeya)
bookshop

la tienda de ultramarinos
(la teeyenda day ultramareenos)
grocery shop

The post office and bank

Carmen and Miguel are at their local post office (correos y telégrafos).

¿Cuánto cuesta enviar este paquete?
(Cwanto cwesta enbeeyar estay pakettay?)
How much is it to send this parcel?

¿A dónde?
(Ah donday?)
Where to?

A Inglaterra.
(Ah Inglaterra.)
To England.

If you want to post letters abroad, look for a letter-box marked 'extranjero'.

Now Carmen is telephoning a friend. When the Spanish answer the telephone they say 'dígame'.

¡Dígame! ¿Quién habla?
(Deegamay! Keeyen abla?)
Hello! Who's speaking?

Soy Carmen. ¿Puedo hablar con Teresa, por favor?
(Soy Carmen. Pweddo ablah con Teressa por fabbor?)
It's Carmen. May I speak to Teresa please?

el dinero
(el dinerro)
money

el banco
(el banco)
bank

la moneda
(la monedda)
coin

la carta
(la carta)
letter

la tarjeta postal
(la tarhetta postal)
postcard

Post office and bank words

correos y telégrafos
(corrayos ee telaygrafos)
post office

por avión   **número de teléfono**
(por abyon)   *(noomerro day telayfono)*
airmail   telephone number

Te llamo más tarde.   **enviar**
(Tay yammo mass tarday.)   *(enbeeyar)*
I'll call you back later.   to send

extranjero   **el tipo de cambio**
(extranherro)   *(el teepo day cambyo)*
foreign   exchange rate

Señor González has gone to the bank to change some euros into English pounds and pence.

¿A cuánto está la libra?
(Ah cwanto esta la leebra?)
How many euros are there to the pound?

el sello
(el seyo)
stamp

el billete
(el beeyettay)
note

el paquete
(el pakettay)
parcel

el teléfono
(el telayfono)
telephone

la tarjeta de crédito
(la tarhetta day creditto)
credit card

Eating out

The González family often has Sunday lunch at a friendly local restaurant.

el pescado
(el peskaddo)
fish

la paella
(la pie-ayah)
paella

el camarero
(el cammarerro)
waiter

La cuenta, por favor.
(La cwenta, por fabbor.)
The bill, please.

¡Aquí lo tiene!
(Akee lo teeyennay!)
Here it is!

¡Buen provecho!
(Bwen probbecho!)
Enjoy your meal!

¿Está bueno?
(Esta bwenno?)
Is it good?

Sí. Está muy rico.
(See. Esta mwee reeko.)
Yes. It's very tasty.

¿Me puedes pasar la sal?
(May pweddess passar la sal?)
Could you pass me the salt?

¡Tengo hambre!
(Tengo ambray!)
I'm hungry!

¡Tengo sed!
(Tengo sed!)
I'm thirsty!

la tortilla de patatas
(la torteeya day patattas)
Spanish omelette

una taza de café
(oona tatha day caffay)
a cup of coffee

una jarra de agua
(oona harra day agwa)
a jug of water

Visiting places

Spain is famous for its sunshine and sandy beaches. As well as going to the seaside, the González family also likes to visit old Spanish castles and small white-washed villages.

el esquí acuático
(el eskee akwattico)
water skiing

¡Vamos a bañarnos!
(Bammoss ah banyarnoss!)
Let's go for a swim!

el mar
(el mar)
sea

la arena
(la arenna)
sand

la lancha neumática
(la lancha newmattica)
rubber dinghy

la playa
(la ply-ya)
beach

¡Hace calor!
(Athay callor!)
It's hot!

la pala
(la palla)
spade

el cubo
(el coobo)
bucket

la sombrilla
(la sombreeya)
sunshade

el balón
(el ballon)
ball

la toalla
(la towalya)
towel

¿Es antiguo aquel castillo?
(Ess anteegwo akel casteeyo?)
Is that castle old?

Sí. Es muy antiguo.
(See. Ess mwee anteegwo)
Yes. It's very old.

Useful visiting words

el partido de fútbol
(el parteedo day footbol)
football match

el parque de atracciones
(el parkay day attrakthyonness)
fairground

el centro turístico
(el thentro turistico)
tourist centre

el palacio
(el palathee-o)
palace

el castillo
(el casteeyo)
castle

la película
(la paylikoola)
film

las cuevas
(las cwebbas)
caves

el teatro
(el tayattro)
theatre

el circo
(el theerko)
circus

la obra de teatro
(la obbra day tayattro)
play

el museo
(el moossayo)
museum

el cine
(el theenay)
cinema

¡Qué bonito es este pueblo!
(Kay boneeto ess estay pweblo!)
This village is pretty!

la gimnasia
(la gymnassiya)
gymnastics

el fútbol
(el footbol)
football

el patinaje
(el patteenahay)
skating

la natación
(la nattathyon)
swimming

el cricket
(el cricket)
cricket

la equitación
(la ekeetathyon)
riding

el windsurf
(el windsoorf)
windsurfing

Carmen and Miguel have met up with some of their friends in the local park.

¿A qué estáis jugando?
(Ah kay estayiss hoogando?)
What are you playing?

A béisbol.
(Ah basebol.)
Baseball.

¿Cómo se juega? ¿Es difícil?
(Como say hwegga? Ess difeetheel?)
How do you play? Is it difficult?

No. Es fácil.
(No. Ess fatheel.)
No. It's easy.

¿Me dejáis jugar?
(May dayhayiss hoogar?)
Can I play?

¡Claro! Necesitamos dieciocho personas.
(Klaroh! Nethesitamos deeyetheeocho personas.)
Of course! We need eighteen people.

el juego del escondite
(el hweggo del eskondeetay)
hide and seek

el ping-pong
(el ping-pong)
ping-pong

22

la pesca
(la peska)
fishing

practicar el remo
(practicah el remo)
rowing

el ciclismo
(el thikleesmo)
cycling

el judo
(el hoodo)
judo

el esquí
(el eskee)
skiing

el footing
(el footing)
jogging

el tenis
(el tennis)
tennis

el golf
(el golf)
golf

el baloncesto
(el balonthesto)
basketball

¿Dónde está la pelota?
(Donday esta la pelota?)
Where is the ball?

¡Está aquí!
(Esta akee!)
It's here!

¡Te toca a ti!
(Tay tocca ah tee!)
Your turn!

el poste
(el postay)
post

¡Tengo sueño!
(Tengo swenyo!)
I'm tired!

el palo
(el pallo)
bat

Accidents and illnesses

The González family keeps all its emergency telephone numbers near the telephone. In Spain there are different numbers for police, ambulance and fire emergencies.

¡Socorro!
(Socorro!)
Help!

¡Fuego!
(Fweggo!)
Fire!

Accident words

¡Cuidado!
(Cweedaddo!)
Watch out!

el coche de la policía
(el cochay day la politheeya)
police car

la urgencia
(la urgentheeya)
emergency

¡Han entrado a robar en mi habitación!
(An entraddo ah robah en mee abitathyon!)
My room has been burgled!

la herida
(la ereeda)
injury

¡Me han robado el bolso!
(May an robaddo el bolso!)
My handbag has been stolen!

la ambulancia
(la ambulantheeya)
ambulance

¡Vengan pronto!
(Bengan pronto!)
Come quickly!

¡Me han robado el billetero!
(May an robaddo el beeyeterro!)
My wallet has been stolen!

Illness words

Tengo una erupción.
(Tengo oona erroopthyon.)
I have a rash.

la tirita
(la tireeta)
sticking plaster

¡Tengo fiebre!
(Tengo feeyebbray!)
I have a temperature!

Tengo dolor de muelas.
(Tengo dollor day mwellas.)
I have a toothache.

el dentista
(el denteesta)
dentist

Tengo algo en el ojo.
(Tengo algo en el o-ho.)
I have something in my eye.

Travelling

The González family is driving to the railway station. They are all meeting some friends from Madrid.

On the way, the family stops the car for some more petrol.

¿Dónde está la estación de servicio más cercana?
(Donday esta la estathyon day serbeethyo mass thercanna?)
Where is the nearest petrol station?

Todo recto.
(Toddo recto.)
Straight on.

la taquilla
(la takeeya)
ticket office

la consigna
(la consinya)
left luggage office

la sala de espera
(la salla day esperra)
waiting room

¿Dónde está la taquilla?
(Donday esta la takeeya?)
Where is the ticket office?

¿A qué hora llega el tren de Madrid?
(Ah kay orra yega el tren day Madrid?)
At what time does the train from Madrid arrive?

A las once.
(Ah las onthay.)
At eleven o'clock.

Detrás de usted.
(Detras day oosted.)
Behind you.

You can find out more about how to say the time in Spanish by looking at page 28.

Later, the friends go into the town centre by themselves.

¿Dónde está la parada del autobús para el centro ciudad?
(Donday esta la paradda del owtobooss parra el thentro thoodad?)
Where is the bus stop for the town centre?

Está aquí.
(Esta akee.)
It's here.

bajarse
(baharsay)
to get off

el pasajero
(el passaherro)
passenger

subirse
(soobeersay)
to get on

Travelling words

coger el autobús
(cohair el owtobooss)
to catch the bus

el billete de ida y vuelta
(el beeyettay day eeda ee bwelta)
return ticket

el billete
(el beeyettay)
ticket

el mapa
(el mappa)
map

el camión
(el camyon)
lorry

dirección única
(dirrekthyon oonika)
one way

la calle
(la kaiyay)
street

el coche
(el cochay)
car

coger el tren
(cohair el tren)
to catch the train

reservar un asiento
(reserbar oon asseeyento)
to reserve a seat

el autocar
(el owtocar)
coach

el jefe de tren
(el heffay day tren)
guard

el tren
(el tren)
train

el andén
(el anden)
platform

perder el tren
(perdair el tren)
to miss the train

More useful words

Time

The Spanish do not use the words 'past' or 'to' when they tell the time. Instead, they use the words 'and' (y), or 'less' (menos).

¿Qué hora es, por favor?
(Kay orra ess, por fabbor?)
What time is it, please?

Son las cinco.
(Son las thinko.)
It is five o'clock.

Son las cinco y diez.
(Son las thinko ee deeyeth.)
It is ten past five.

Son las cinco y cuarto.
(Son las thinko ee cwarto.)
It is quarter past five.

Son las cinco y media.
(Son las thinko ee medya.)
It is half past five.

Son las seis menos cuarto.
(Son las seys mennos cwarto.)
It is quarter to six.

Es mediodía.
(Ess medyodee-a.)
It is midday.

Es medianoche.
(Ess medyanochay.)
It is midnight.

Times of the day

la tarde
(la tarday)
afternoon

la noche
(la nochay)
night

la mañana
(la manyanna)
morning

la tarde
(la tarday)
evening (early)

la noche
(la nochay)
evening (late)

28

The months of the year and days of the week

The Spanish do not use capital letters at the beginning of the names of the months or the days of the week.

enero
(enerro)
January

febrero
(febrerro)
February

marzo
(martho)
March

abril
(abreel)
April

mayo
(mayo)
May

junio
(hooneeyo)
June

julio
(hooleeyo)
July

agosto
(agosto)
August

septiembre
(septyembray)
September

octubre
(octoobray)
October

noviembre
(nobbyembray)
November

diciembre
(dithyembray)
December

lunes *(looness)* Monday	**martes** *(martess)* Tuesday	**miércoles** *(meeyercolles)* Wednesday
	jueves *(hwebbess)* Thursday	**viernes** *(beeyernes)* Friday
	sábado *(sabbaddo)* Saturday	**domingo** *(domingo)* Sunday

The seasons

la primavera
(la preemaberra)
spring

el verano
(el beranno)
summer

el otoño
(el ottonyo)
autumn

el invierno
(el inbeeyerno)
winter

Clothes and parts of the body

la camisa
(la cameesa)
shirt

la chaqueta
(la jacketa)
jacket

los pantalones
(los pantaloness)
trousers

los pantalones cortos
(los pantaloness cortos)
shorts

el calcetín
(el calthetin)
sock

la nariz
(la nareeth)
nose

el ojo
(el o-ho)
eye

la cabeza
(la cabbetha)
head

el pelo
(el pello)
hair

la boca
(la bocca)
mouth

la oreja
(la orreha)
ear

el dedo
(el deddo)
finger

la blusa
(la bloosa)
blouse

el cuello
(el cweyo)
neck

el mentón
(el menton)
chin

el hombro
(el ombro)
shoulder

la muñeca
(la munyeka)
wrist

la falda
(la falda)
skirt

el brazo
(el bratho)
arm

el codo
(el codo)
elbow

la mano
(la manno)
hand

la rodilla
(la roddeeya)
knee

el vestido
(el besteedo)
dress

la pierna
(la peeyerna)
leg

el tobillo
(el tobeeyo)
ankle

el pie
(el peeyay)
foot

el pulóver
(el pullover)
pullover

el abrigo
(el abreego)
coat

el dedo del pie
(el deddo del peeyay)
toe

el zapato
(el thapato)
shoe

30

Colours and numbers

1 uno *(oono)*

2 dos *(doss)*

3 tres *(tres)*

4 cuatro *(cwattro)*

5 cinco *(thinko)*

6 seis *(seys)*

7 siete *(syettay)*

8 ocho *(ocho)*

9 nueve *(nwebbay)*

10 diez *(deeyeth)*

11 once *(onthay)*

12 doce *(dothay)*

13 trece *(trethay)*

14 catorce *(catorthay)*

15 quince *(kinthay)*

16 dieciséis *(deeyetheeseys)*

17 diecisiete *(deeyetheesyettay)*

18 dieciocho *(deeyetheeocho)*

19 diecinueve *(deeyetheenwebbay)*

amarillo *(ammareeyo)* yellow

naranja *(narranha)* orange

rojo *(ro-ho)* red

verde *(berday)* green

azul *(athool)* blue

blanco *(blanco)* white

negro *(neggro)* black

rosa *(rossa)* pink

gris *(greess)* grey

marrón *(marron)* brown

Underneath is the Spanish verb **tener**, to have.

tengo *(tengo)* I have

tienes *(teeyennes)* you have (familiar singular)

tiene *(teeyennay)* you have (polite singular) he/she/it has

tenemos *(tenemmos)* we have

tenéis *(tennayiss)* you have (familiar plural)

tienen *(teeyennen)* you have (polite plural) they have

---

20 veinte *(beyntay)*

21 veintiuno *(beynteeoono)*

22 veintidós *(beynteedoss)*

30 treinta *(treynta)*

40 cuarenta *(cwarenta)*

50 cincuenta *(thinkwenta)*

60 sesenta *(sessenta)*

70 setenta *(setenta)*

80 ochenta *(ochenta)*

90 noventa *(nobbenta)*

100 cien *(theeyen)*

1,000 mil *(meel)*

1,000,000 un millón *(oon meeyon)*

el cocodrilo
(el cocodreelo)
crocodile

Animals

la ballena
(la bayena)
whale

el oso
(el osso)
bear

el delfín
(el delfeen)
dolphin

la cebra
(la thebra)
zebra

la gorila
(la goreela)
gorilla

el lobo
(el lobo)
wolf

la panda
(la panda)
panda

el tigre
(el tigray)
tiger

el león
(el layon)
lion

There are two verbs meaning 'to be' in Spanish. **Ser** is used to describe people and things and for telling the time.

soy
(soy)
I am

somos
(somoss)
we are

eres
(erress)
you are (familiar singular)

sois
(soyis)
you are (familiar plural)

es
(ess)
you are (polite singular)
he/she/it is

son
(son)
you are (polite plural)
they are

Estar is used to say where people and things are (eg 'She is in the dining room.'). It is also used to describe something that will not last long (eg 'It is snowing.').

estoy
(estoy)
I am

estamos
(estammos)
we are

estás
(estas)
you are (familiar singular)

estáis
(estayiss)
you are (familiar plural)

está
(esta)
you are (polite singular)
he/she/it is

están
(estan)
you are (polite plural)
they are

el canguro
(el kangooroo)
kangaroo

el elefante
(el elefantay)
elephant

la jirafa
(la heeraffa)
giraffe